Dry Stone Work

Also by Brian Johnstone

POETRY
The Book of Belongings (Arc Publications, 2009)
Homing (The Lobby Press, 2004)
Robinson, A Journey (Akros Publications, 2000)
The Lizard Silence (Scottish Cultural Press, 1996)

POETRY IN TRANSLATION
Terra Incognita (L'Officina (Vincenza) 2009)

AS EDITOR
The Memory of Fields: the poetry of Mark Ogle
(Akros Publications, 2000)
The Golden Goose Hour (Taranis Books, 1994)

BRIAN JOHNSTONE

Dry Stone Work

Arc
PUBLICATIONS

2014

Published by Arc Publications
Nanholme Mill, Shaw Wood Road
Todmorden OL14 6DA, UK
www.arcpublications.co.uk

Design by Tony Ward

Printed in Great Britain by TJ International, Padstow, Cornwall

978 1908376 05 3 (pbk)
978 1908376 06 0 (hbk)

ACKNOWLEDGEMENTS

Thanks are due to the editors of the following publications in which several poems (or earlier versions) have appeared: *New Writing Scotland, Gutter, Causeway / Cabhsair, Chapman, Magma, Reactions (4), Revival, Fourteen, Island, Northwords Now, Markings, New Writing Dundee, Poetry Greece* and The Writers' Bureau journal. Various poems have appeared in the anthologies *100 Favourite Scottish Poems* (Luath, 2006), *Such Strange Joy* (iynx, 2001) and *Split Screen* (Red Squirrel Press, 2012) and on the Ink, Sweat & Tears, Magma, Translation Lab, The Drunken Boat, The Open Mouse, The Poetry Kit & Scottish Poetry Library websites.

Translations of various poems were published in *Post Scriptum* (Sweden, translator Boel Schenlaer), and *La Otra 12* (Mexico, translators Victor Rodriguez Nunez & Katherine M. Hedeen). 'Parable' first appeared in the fine art folio *Postcard* (Dundee Printmakers, 1998). 'Storm Chaser' was featured in the exhibition Dualism (Chris Park, 2010-11). 'Surfin' Safari for a Small Town Boy' was a prize-winner in the National Poetry Competition in 2000; 'Reservoir' won the Writers' Bureau Poetry Competition in 2002; 'Blanket' was a prize-winner in the Poetry on the Lake Competition in 2003; 'Tree Surgeons' was long-listed for the Magma Competition 2011 and selected for the Scottish Poetry Library's online anthology *Best Scottish Poems 2011*. Both 'Who Knew' and 'How Well It Burns' were commissioned, the former for the anthology *Split Screen*, the latter for the filmpoem project *Absent Voices*.

Thanks are also due to the Scottish Arts Council (now Creative Scotland) for the award of a Professional Development Grant (2010).

Cover image by Will Maclean

Editor for the UK and Ireland: John W. Clarke

for Jean

Contents

HEARTINGS

COPINGS

The stones we writers use are words. As we hold them in our hands, sensing the ways in which each of them is connected to the others, looking at them sometimes from afar, sometimes almost caressing them with our fingers and the tips of our pens, weighing them, moving them around, year in and year out, patiently and hopefully, we create new worlds.

ORHAN PAMUK
Nobel Prize in Literature acceptance speech,
December 2006

FOOTINGS

Tobacco Road

when every man jack lit up no-one expected worse

a shortness of puff
dry hoast
fingers stained lino brown

and that tobacco breath overall air
meant these men were men

there in their place

feet on the rail
slops pooling the top of the bar and something they'd all made
their fathers' their grandfathers' smoke
tinting the walls

the sweat of their work
still pocking the ceiling with dots

where the reek had condensed and dripped off

like their lives
truncated by work

slid like a nip down the length of the bar

and lost in the smoke
that fizzled from nostrils as the tip of each roll up
glowed

The Thousand Blows

What's done to wood cannot be
undone; to steel
abrasives can rub down,

a whetstone can restore,
and could with time
this edge

that hasn't seen its like
for years. The thousand blows
this handle took,

shivered in the splintered grain,
splits so old
they've taken on

the patina of age, the tally
of time spent
over chisel, over bench

where cord was little use
to bind the stock,
damaged by the hefted knock,

no more than
accident deferred. It's held
but would not do

for long. This long. As long
as steel is dull,
the edge unused,

the rust grown slowly
on the blade,
the sweat that soaked

into the handle
with each blow glowing
in the dim electric light

that aids a rummage
in the drawer where each one
of the thousands

has its twin
in other blows, in other tools
forgotten as the men

who made them
sing. Let them lie here, goods
no-one will get

the good of, ends as rough
as hands that held them,
weary with it all.

Reservoir

Something tolls, dead in the water,
from sixty years back; chimes
in the stonework of the brain

the way a mother's voice is never
quite forgotten, the sounds of childhood
carry through somehow. And you

look downwards at the brink, knowing
that the eddies washing on this shore
have inhabited what's left of life

that quit this valley by decree.
The banking stretches out behind you;
notices on poles advise against

a list of things from which the years
have cut you off, the way these waters have
from house and plot, familiar homes,

the chapel where you pumped the organ
for the psalms. Ignored, the gables rise
like bibles in a rack from where

you always knew they would, in time.
And now the drought has dropped
the level of the water twenty feet, enough

to recognise where lanes had been,
how houses all had hunkered in together,
formed the township that you left

to which you have returned, a memory
in someone else's book: an old man
staring out across this reservoir, as deep

in thought as are the sounds
of church bells, accents, running water,
steeped in sixty years of loss.

Dry Stone Work

Teamwork, you said and grabbed the corner
of the sack.
             Too late. My tensing back,
unused like yours to working with its hands,
went crack, as strain was felt and slack
was taken up. We soldiered on and stones
built thick and fast. Time dribbled past
and you, my senior by a score of years,
worked steadfast hour on hour. I gasped
and, fighting to keep up, the stones became
this wall.
           Now, looking at it all,
you off to more jobs still to do, it seems
a small thing to have made me crawl
from chair to chair, with aching back,
feeling much as stones inside a sack.

Ghost Story

Studded with ghosts, this whinstone wall
proves each one in a nail rusted into mortar,
where roses hang blood red or spectral white.

Their petals fall like generations who took care
to hammer iron into stone until each climber,
like a family tree, criss-crossed the wall.

Now left to us, still fast in cracks, are siblings
we must try to link with rose stems of our own,
to tie them to the present if our reach allows.

It fails for some, and those ignored we cannot
make the stretch to, gaze useless at us, distant
bare accusers, stonewalled, stranded in their time.

The Tattie Line

In '65 the last train passed, enthusiasts aboard,
notebooks and sharpened pencils making their farewells
to a line no-one had seen fit ever to finish

but left, truncated in the upland farms,
its junction projected but never reached, the coast
an aspiration war and lack of manpower rendered void.

Complete, its fate would not have differed;
needs had changed. The Tattie Line – the name
men knew it by – never grew into its function which is now,

abandoned as it is, to carry not the planned for crops
but wildlife, native flowers – a strip of set-aside
before the term was coined – deep into the spine of Fife,

a backbone split where bridges have been taken down,
a cutting has been filled with stones, a field
has spread its edge, the hint of ballast lingering in the soil,

such that today you'd scarcely know the route
without a map, its memory a barely noticed dotted line
the OS sheet tags TK of old RLY: this Ariadne's thread.

Concrete Poem

The ghosts of men who haunt this track
won't fade the way their footprints in the dust
are driven off by wind or rain. For men

it surely was, whose urgent need
to get to fields and flocks trumped every sign
for drying concrete, drove their boots and trucks

across the still-to-set but hardening surface
of the past. A past where traces
of a shovel or a rake are secrets held in stasis

a roadman might detect, while others
see just shadows, creases in the finish of the road;
unlike those flagrant tyre tracks scrawled

from gate to gate. Or these deep scores that tell
of grasping far too late that one man's truck
had sunk up to its axle in the stuff,

sloughed in the footprints of his rescuers;
and this past, this one deed imprinted in the place
as clear as time will print its passing in a face.

The Ring Cycle

I

WHIP HAND

Believing in the possibility
of showtime
that the sound of circus music blaring

from the speakers on the roof
means more
than silver in my pocket, pegs to hammer home,

I stake out another pitch and flatten grass:
for what?
The cheers, the hollow gasps, the silence

as I place my head inside each
lion's mouth.
It's not the teeth, the jaws I fear but seeing

deep into their eyes, each pupil blank
as every pitch
we quit, lifeless as the ground we pack so hard.

THE DIVIDING LINE

Silence – you insist on it –
takes you by the throat,
forces you to breathe

as each step hangs you
in the balance,
draws you to the line.

From there to here
the wire divides
the air above the ring,

cuts failure from success.
No net is your style,
your small vanity, proof

of something that
your hands stretch out
to touch, grip light

in cruciform, upon the pole.
Out there tomorrow
looms up on the far side

of today. Tomorrow where
they stretch the wire again
and you step into time.

III

Heft

Once he was the bee's knees, the very donkey;
cock of the walk, he could wow them all,
straining every fibre till his veins stood out
like cables, hefting what he would later stow

one-handed. A struggle to feign an effort,
hauling until the prentice boys called him
for what he was – for what they all were,
faking their way from pitch to pitch, rattling

the tin. A prop apiece; his the show of strength,
the hups and heave-hos he'd let fly each night,
sly as the skin he knew had changed its spots:
the leopard's pelt he'd slip into before the show

to take his torso – oiled and gleaming – out
into the lights. The band would play, drums
would roll, the punters loose a gasp. And he
would dare to stare distrust full in the eye.

IV

A STUDIED FALL

My feet are growing into these shoes, my hair
into this wig. More than the flesh I was born with,

red rubber becomes my nose. Douse me in gloop,
plant a pie in my face, then I'm real. Trip me up

so I fall like a fool, I'm that fool, one all the punters
dread. Ghost of their blunders, shade of their gaffes,

I'm the spectre that haunts their conceit. Spilt milk
is all I evoke in this gear, icon of mockery done up

in motley and slap. Priest at the altar, prostrate
in the ring, I'm face down in the sawdust, my ritual

redeeming their fall. Under the pancake I blush
to my roots, feel my grease-painted eyebrows rise.

v

Long Shot

It's primed and ready for the off. Stock rigged,
positioned, checked for glitches, flaws. The angle
of trajectory exact, net tensed and stretched,

the whole shebang all set to launch its prize
right across expectant air. She knows full well
they chose her for her size, her slight build

an advantage they can not afford to do without,
her background in the shows as fitting for the road
as could be hoped. She loves the job, she's not afraid

to own to anyone; loves the ever pregnant pause
before the cannon's shot; loves the rush, the sheer hit
of the act, the heights she never would have gained

left to herself. Bang goes the gun and she's a trace
of smoke, a passing blur that was herself, projectile
in the moment that it takes, as mad for it as ever

as she hits the spot they'd worked out for her
in the prep. Job done, she bounces to her feet
and bowing, snaffles the applause like meat.

A Certain Swing

The climb will rest her mind. Hand over hand,
it takes her closer to the bar. One hundred stares,

the chances that she's open to, all pick her out,
a posed apotheosis stretching for the space,

the air she steps out into, taking with her
nothing but her skill. Her trust is in the game.

It is no game. As serious as love she moves
in arcs, censer at a liturgy. The crowd believes

in miracles; she in time. One on one they meet,
a moment not too soon. Her hands are there,

his take them, grasp on grasp, hand over hand.

The Caring Blade

Hooded, blind, I'm stood
against a wall. Vile things
that look to happen to me
never do. He slips them in
a millimetre, less, from flesh
that's learned never to flinch,
never to quiver. I feel them,
all the cool blades slip about
my limbs, caress my cheeks
with no more than a rush
of air as they, in series, find
their mark. Then he's blind
too. A gasp as once again
his arm is raised, the knives
propelled and I, their target,
not even once emit a sigh,
a groan. I'm left alone since
he's the one who takes it all:
the cheers, the mad applause,
the whistles, cries and roars
he's due. Me too, I think, but
it is not to be. I slip the hood,
step down and quit the ring.
It's his thing now. He's king.

PITCH

He hangs from a hook on the back of a door,
his trailer empty without him. Top hat
and tail coat, britches and whip, he's all there

though his spirit is off in a bar, by the docks,
by the station, on the far side of town. He's trying
to see out the show, keep enough of himself

in the place that it counts, giving his life
to the road. No-one knows him, he thinks,
this far from the pitch, this far from the boasting,

the crying of acts, the touting of improbabilities
he's the ringmaster of. Put the hat on his head,
the clothes on his back, place the whip

in a gloved right hand. All that he needs
is his voice to sound true. The voice he is seeking
in a bottle, a glass, those rings he's left on the table.

Sonny Rollins on the Williamsburg Bridge

This is a private place. I can blow my horn as loud as I want.
SONNY ROLLINS

Someone had heard you up there, riffing
amongst the girders, rhythm-synching
with the trains, gulls rising in the updraft
of your breath. *It's beautiful*, you said,

in all its emptiness – that expanse of bridge,
your passage to the silence that the city
took away. Two blocks from your apartment,
the walkway had drawn you up, called you

to take the stand. Its vacancy enticing,
the space you need to grow is somewhere
in the steel, the leaden sky. Case in hand,
you shamble towards the apex, stoop

and take your sax out of the plush, slot
neck to horn, and tongue the reed. The kid
who'd doorstepped Hawk for just a scrawl,
who'd trained up in the closet at his folks',

blowing the changes out there on the span,
in space you never quite came back from,
(as the guys all said, not knowing what
to look for, you'd been shedding for so long);

seeking the notes you felt you could deliver,
bigger than your name. And can do now,
alone here, high above the slow East River,
deep and blue and choppy like your song.

after the film Who is Sonny Rollins? *by Dick Fontaine*

The Method

I was a child nobody wanted. A lonely girl with a dream...
MARILYN MONROE

There are ways of acting which can be taught;
if the actor uses The Method

it will look a lot like real life. It may even
start to feel like that. It is as plausible as a dream.

She wasn't an orphan. She had a mother,
had a father, living in a mansion in Beverly Hills.

Sometimes she thinks: *if I was pretty enough,
my father would come and take me away.*

In the orphanage she stares through the window
at the distant neon

on top of the RKO lot,
sees it flash and thinks, *someday.*

A Method actor will do something false
until it becomes second nature. That way

they will not be playing at it. No-one
will be able to tell the difference. Perhaps the actor

will not be able to tell the difference either.
Sometimes, if a life is awful enough,

there will be comfort in this. A doctor says: *Child,
save your tears! You may need them.*

from the writing of Alastair McKay

TRACINGS

Dolls' House Skies

This girl is a housekeeper
in tissue and card,
a curtain maker in Christmas paper,

a layer of carpet and rug
in scraps of torn fabric, my time.
Her tables grow chairs,

beds bedside tables
scaled to approximate size
for inhabitants turned on their sides

as thus lie her bears
limbs jointed and gesturing sagely
at dolls' house skies.

And I, as she says, *a good spying boy,*
her foil of the moment,
am crouched in the wood

searching the leaf mould and moss
for acorn saucers and cups,
for something I'd lost.

Making the Change

Each third of a pint
was passed round the class
till all

had their bottle and paper straw,
a hole poked into the foil,
and time to suck

the warm as blood,
or chilled from frosty mornings
goodness

governments they'd never heard of
put their way. One extra,
two or three

if more were absent,
made the rounds, an object lesson
in the doing,

in the agitating
all were urged to do
to churn the stuff to butter, fresh

as their amazement
at the trick. The solid,
chilled and spread on biscuits,

oozed and crunched on gappy teeth,
imaginations sparked
and harking back

to frozen bottles, winter crystals
icy on the gums,
the mystery of transformation,

milk persuading them of change.

On the Site of the Southside Joke Shop

Where we stood is long gone, victim
of the wrecking ball, the mell and drill,

but still the faint aroma of amusement
lingers on the pavement, an echo

of the flower, forever false, that hides
its jet of water in a pistil; the rubber egg

that tries to emulate an over easy fry
to fool the unaware. It's there we bought

the ready-made concoction that itched
its targets into paroxysms of desire

to tear their clothes off, scratch until
their skin was raw, our eyes wept

with the jape of it; there we picked up
phial bombs full of schoolboy stinks

to slyly roll below a desk, waiting for
the random foot, unwary, unsuspecting,

to shatter one, and let the joke of nausea
flow out like the hysterics it produced

in grown-ups not *au fait* with all the fun
of smells. Long gone, but its plate glass

holds reflections in the mind. Behind
its freshly polished shine, the whoopees,

how's-your-fathers, woops-a-daisy joys
of slippy, smirking, up and under boys.

Surfin' Safari for a Small Town Boy

The best pop is like a rush of lust.
                                    ALASTAIR MCKAY

The deuce coupe threads the dunes, back of the sands:
her daddy's car, but he will understand

that parties must be seized, she says, like days,
thrown as hand-made pots, agreed the way

they've signed their surfboards, waxed them down
like documents. In this grey town

the sounds of doo-wop only surface from the drains
that overflow, the malice of late summer rains

determined in their pock-marked progress
over sands and shallows, all that acned skin, to mess

up every wrung out joy that they display,
gleaming in convertibles: the Wilsons, Jardine, Love, gay

in some forgotten sense. The discs stack up,
the portable Dansette slaps platter on to platter, enough

to wind the Provost up, his bike a solitary patrol
against the shameless pleasure of it all.

Awful in his cycle clips, flat cap, he gets around, his face
a sucked in breath of disapproval. Go on, chase

the blues away before he gets on to your back.
The surf is up. The wind is from the north. But fuck,

all summer long this is as good as it will get. The needle
hits the groove. Love's voice. You paddle

out beyond the waves, youth tied on with a cord.
She watches you, God only knows, holds your reward

in supple limbs. You feel the surge. You sing it. Sea
rips at your board. She says: *Sing it one more time for me.*

Storm Chaser

The wind holds you up
only so long as you can stand it.
Stand the dark and it will surprise you.

Palms genuflect. Fenders and trash cans
surrender themselves. A trailer
kicks ass against a wall, shatters.

You stand it, stand in it,
shout into your miked-up means
of holding on to something, pinning down

the fact that all it threw at you
went by. Rain Gatling guns the main street,
tarmac seethes like insect life.

And this one, as you rock it out
behind a wall, pumps twister after twister
through the climate in your veins.

Who Knew

People are quite happy believing the wrong things.
Tom Baker

Seen first on the floor of UNIT prone, a miasma
of black and white, that smile not yet in evidence
as the credits rolled, his new form firmed up.

Regeneration absolute, the smile filled up a screen
where interference passed for SFX, jelly babies
were a metaphor for nothing worse than glee.

That scarf too, only some mad simile for DNA,
and topped by floppy curls that any latent hippy
would've died for – if they'd spoken like that then.

The Doctor couldn't do it, couldn't die, grappled
every cliff-hanger and grinned them out unfazed:
no plastic alien, cardboard spaceship ever up to him.

What was he on, we wondered, seriously stoned,
as the '70s progressed unchecked? That lit-up smile
betokened more than on-another-planet, man.

Out of the box? No way. The TARDIS flew him
off through time and space, dimensions relative
to those we tracked him by – the box we turned on

weekly, watched flicker in a moment back to life.

Lady Day's Experience

What was music to our ears, she said,
was too much

grief to hers – the broken voice
of Lady Day's experience

leaking from the room
our youth was filling with a hunger

for that bit more
than rock or bubble gum.

We hadn't noticed
as the door had opened, she'd come in

weeping into one last glass of wine;
the woman she still was,

(no way his take-for-granted mum)
had shown us both

how Billie's damaged vocal chords
corralled the blues

to open wounds that comfort
couldn't close.

An unexpected pain
had seeped out of the grooves,

shocked us so much that we changed
the record as she asked.

A woman's voice, another's
bitter tears that aged us, playing cool

in that suburban room, taught us so much
more than liner notes reveal.

As From a Car

The way you see this side of life is always
from a car: rained on and out of focus;
wiper blades in motion slicing images
apart; drops of scuzzy drizzle blotting out
the view. Dim light shows a line of pylons,
road signs flashing past; night a glimpse
of open ground where someone's lit a fire;
and the distances between us all are squared.

Weather beats its long tattoo on surfaces
we've manufactured, polished up
to show us as we wish to be, assured
of one thing, where we drive and when
has as little bearing on where we plan to stop
as does the glare of someone's headlights
flaring in the mirror, the white lines men
have staggered down the centre of the road.

To Live Apart

That faint booming as cars coast across the bridge,
the ravenous slap of wind on glass
conspire to turn my thoughts in one direction:

your going. A night like any might have been
before you crossed the road, waited for the lift
that you'd been taking there for years. I watched you go,

dividing in my mind the spoils, taking
pictures from their nails, photographs from frames
that later, in the garage, I would break. The images

I kept, buried them beneath the surface of my days,
below the passports, door keys, airline tickets,
beneath the scars.

The tissue heals, knits back. The fabric of the mind
repairs itself. I listen, waiting at the corner of the road,
wondering, what was that sound?

Parable

in an effort at reconciliation he offered her a fish

the fish itself was compliant
being out of its element it had little choice

allowing the scales to fall was easy
they were of little consequence
one by one they scattered like a crowd dispersed

between them the fish lay on its paper
prone

the knife was an afterthought
having nothing to do with her hands she seized upon it
in haste

the blade was sharp
her mind studied it by degrees

solemnly the dead eye of the fish regarded them

not to be outdone he made as if to speak
the emptiness of his mouth betrayed him in a hollow O

the fish grinned in silence

with one deft stroke
she slid the blade below the bone

Codicil

Those years
    torn down the middle
split from the membrane
       a scribble
across the feint
rest like the trace of a vein
       blue
on the back of a hand
      barely there.

But there in the memory
of words
    gulped back
to the hollow below the tongue
eased
   from the coils of the brain
and slated to fade.

Like the spine of a book
      exposed to sun
a dress
   washed once too often
or a photograph
      someone forgot to fix
now
blank and bobbing
     dank in the tray.

Contracted

My other hand is turning now,
twisting and knotting

beneath the skin
with this small affliction they say

came down through the Vikings –
so slowly the changes

seem almost in geological time
but it's happening

even so. I can feel my finger
ratchetting down,

my hand imperceptibly cupping,
forming a fist.

The clues are there –
a callus where none can be, tissue

ridged like bone. It is pulling
as I sleep. I'm in need

of the knife whose hard stare split
my other grip

years back. The proof –
a furrow, settled, healed to a scar

that tracks from print to palm, and
bedded in the skin

an afterthought,
a single stitch, forgotten, overlooked –

this dot of blue
I thought might be a period, a stop.

Blanket

It flops down from the cupboard shelf by chance,
the grey of something needing to be spread
again on earth, below taut canvas, half
remembered sky. Still hinting at the smoke
of memories, it slumps like wood ash now
beneath my feet, green blanket-stitch the moss
on stones placed round a fire.
                                        And glowing red?
A name tag tacking this to me, to years
in single figures, summer camps in fields
ploughed over when the tents were razed and gone;
the imprint of the past like patterns left
by grass stems in the flesh of knees,
                                              that fade
as skin is stretched in standing, walking tall.

Back at Bash Street

He's grilling a kipper he's pronged on a fork
in front of the staffroom fire. His missus,

she's dropped him right in it again, gone off
to her mother's – left him to cope. Next frame

he's discovered and mocked. He's forgotten
the kids he'd told to report and they find him

alone with his tea. Lonely old Teacher, quite
down in the mouth, a martyr to ulcers and gout,

but fond of red herrings, a pickle or two,
found out by his pupils, the worst of the crew,

who won't let it rest till the end of the strip
when he's sweating in buckets and ready to flip.

Askew

Strange that the eye accepts all this street
can throw at it
with something approaching glee.

Wanting lines, horizontals,
some regularity,
here they're just not to be found.

The abundance of all that's askew
in doorways, window frames,
the slope of a sill

feels like happiness
captured in brick and stone,
the life lines of this old place: eccentric,

a bit off the wall
like someone we all knew
back in our past, but couldn't invent

if we tried. It's made plain
in the age of the buildings, the narrow
twist of the street,

the tug that 500 years' gravity makes
on foundations
more likely laid down for wood,

for the timber framed structures
these houses once were
before fashion stacked Georgian facades

on the faces they show to the world. Now
they slip step the length
of this ridge-top street, arm in arm,

gable to gable: a row of old pals
lined up, somewhat shaky,
but comfy in company, content in their skin.

The Baileys, Durham

HEARTINGS

Reading the Book

Limp-covered, unprotected, paperbacks
have grown their marks the way a body might respond
to wounds in childhood, injury's distress;

grown them from the chop of steel,
the nicks in blades that sheared them square
to leave raised tracks that curve across the page-ends

like a scar. They bear these too: the indentations
pulsed through covers that fade out only
as the plot develops, characters begin to grow. And there

the corners start to crease, each random scalene
waiting for a thumb to smooth it out,
to claim the place back from somebody pausing in a past

which left these pits and scores
by accident, from skill a little less than it might be,
or pressing time, preserved here in the strata of a book.

Zakros

Tales say the first to dig here found
not masonry, remains, but little more than rocks,
a random stash of what the earth had left there,

men had skirted, struck, ploughed over
in the course of daily toil. Tales that foreign schools
were close, were closer than they knew

to what persistence would have brought them to
with time. That time they did not have
but others, coming later in the day, native speakers

talking to the men who farmed the soil, found
just the faintest blush of memory
for potsherds, broken tile, hints at hand-cut blocks

a spade had grazed some early morning
when the air was cool, defining this,
their spot: the palace every clue had brought them to,

each inscription had predicted, long before
its ritual spaces, lobbies, stairs were opened up
to air, to commerce of a different shade, its footfall

treading floors earth loosened from itself
where cisterns, full again with water, harbour reeds
the wind blows time through, sighing as it goes.

Kato Zakros, Crete

Source

Explain this as the guidebooks do,
plant a park around its banks,
put signs up, answer all the questions,

still its mystery remains. Like breath,
the water wells out from the rock
men say is simply porous strata

carrying this river from the distance
to debouch it here below the gaze of what
has marked these depths as sacred

for who knows how many years –
the Virgin nested in the surface of the cliff
quite beyond all access now. Unlike

the wonder of this place: a thin mist
rising from the water, its surface
black and unrewarding to the gaze,

but swelling in the centre of the pool,
receiving by the minute, urging
every molecule of river water up

and on between enclosing rocks,
tributary that it truly is. Even as,
millennia before, receiver too, men

slid its tribute deep into the reaches
of another world, that's here,
still somehow straining to be heard.

Chatillon-sur-Seine, Burgundy

Tokens of Admission

Bound in, the way the foundlings were for permanence,
each strip of cloth is both their future and their past
cut so with blades that one will match the other

should the latter change, the mother find the wherewithal
to make the journey back. Few did, so few that even
one page in a score of scores matched up is rare;

while pattern after pattern, warp and weft, pins
every child nameless to its place, to noted features,
measurements and dates, each mother more than absence:

twill or damask, linen, silk or lace, a sliver of the clothes
the infant wore when circumstance reduced them
to a bundle, a parcel passed on unaddressed.

The Garment District

Evening was always a problem. Sit in the dark
or have someone turn up the gas. She might wave
from the landing – her neighbour would see her,

a figure in shadow expected each Sabbath
as sun left the streets, having long quit the rooms
and the tenement's depths, light needing to fight

its way in. A small obligation: the turning of keys,
match to the mantles, a neighbourly easing of chores
forbidden to families of literal faith. When,

came at nightfall each Friday, ever the same,
such that weeks were pricked out by it, lined up
like the cloth they would all tack together,

dipping their needles in turn. Sharing the graft
of the Lower East Side from daybreak to dusk,
each difference rubbed off like the knap on a suit,

the garments they wore all came to appear
of a piece. Patterns changed quickly, but each end
of the week she stood there and waved, figure

more stout, somewhat stooped, that her neighbour
still sees looking back, as she waits for the light
to fill the apartment stitches have long left behind.

Craiglockhart

Maybe they're here somewhere, lost
in these crowds of students, informal
in their tweeds, plus fours –

Sassoon, the elder, Sunday golfer;
Owen, bookish, gangly, pale – mingling
with the queue for the refectory,

snatching nervously at fags, ignoring
notices forbidding all those here
to smoke. You catch a glimpse

you think, later, in the distance
– backs straight, military haircuts –
turning down a corridor you glance along

but they're not there. No, no-one is, though
low light slants through window frames,
plants these crosses on the wall.

Sappers

Men took them from the light
to understand the dark,

brightness in the chalk
blinding them like snowfields

a single candle would create
in tunnels feet below the trenches

where light would only enter
with ignition as the fuses blew,

fury and the earth itself
would leech in with the lust for gain

that led them crawling day and night,
silent underneath the few

contested yards
they had to talk in whispers in,

catch every loosened pebble
in the damper of their upturned hands,

till snow blind
from the ground they'd undermined

men took them from the dark
to understand the light.

How Well It Burns

How well it burns, the sugar that your parting hands
would throw frustrated on a sulking fire,
its blue flames urging each reluctant coal to life.

You'd gaze at it back then, a world you'd changed
with just one act, drawn into the smoke
that raced towards the sky like all your dreams.

What shape they took, bar flight, you scarce recall,
eyes fixed on dials or peering out at night,
your target not too distant, not too exposed to flak.

The coast is clear. No moon but still the water far below
glistens like molasses, the islands blacker yet
against the estuary you creep up like some sneak.

The turn to east-north-east is unmistakeable, drilled
in maps, in night-flight training as you are;
and there it is. You ease the joy-stick, take her round.

Below, co-ordinates ring true. The oblong of the dock
betrays the sheds, the streets behind them
full of families you must banish from your mind.

How well it burns and will do if you have your way.
The bomb doors disengage like parting hands.
This whole town of sugar must see flame tonight.

The Greenock Blitz, 6th May 1941

68

A Hotel in the Bernese Oberland

It's the days before war in this loft,
but officer class. Trunks line the walls,
tackle and rods, swaddled in canvas,

wait here for their owners' return. Cases,
piled high on the shelves, left for the next
Alpine trip, speak through their labels

of privilege, worn from the leather no-one
has buffed in an age. A once grand hotel
waits for its life to return, the '30s to lift off

again, all the young chaps to come back,
skis on their shoulders, or fishing rods
under their arms, each alpenstock ready

to tackle the routes. Too soon gone,
like vacations, the men we regret, names
on a monument remembered elsewhere,

in a parish, some village church. Their kit
for the season is gathering dust, left here
for the summers they never would see,

the winters whose snows stay untracked,
as the dust on the shelves of this attic
is now, weighing the days since the war.

from the account by Kevin Crossley-Holland

Opening Up the Bag

The kind of bag your mother knocked up
for your plimsolls, is what this item is

but military khaki not the regulation
colours of your school. And inside

not the gym shoes PE staff demanded
for the wall bars and the ropes. Instead

a route through Africa and Italy, grainy
in the black and white of contact prints

that haven't seen the light, it seems,
for years. They track the course of war,

and one man's ordered steps along it
on the road to home, to his own ration

of the nation's thanks. Though dog-eared,
creased and curled with age, each snap

is an assertion that he made it, while
each figure there in all the early frames,

but absent as the pile grows lower,
is proof that others fell by waysides

heaps of soil and crosses hammered up
from scavenged timber mark in maybe

half a dozen prints – the last memento
of a mate who bought it as the war

rolled on. But *he's* there, balding even
at that early age, moustache as clipped

and neat as ever, recognisably the father
he'd become by making it on through

this one-man Med campaign. Its images
unseen while he was just a dad, the war

simply a reference point, a presence
never more than back story, a given

all his generation understood but wouldn't,
couldn't speak of to the next. Till death,

his passing in his sixties, opened up
this story, loosed off the drawstrings

of the bag, let out that younger man,
sergeant in his thirties, to march the route

again, in picture after picture, the family
he lived to make, following his train.

A Disused Cinema in Lithuania

The wood this place is made of, it's returning to.
Study the base of the beams; the timber
is papery, soft and smelling of earth.

As strange as its site, is this lettering: art deco!
but fashioned by hand, all of its stylised swoosh
insisting on glamour, pizzazz,

although here in this forest the words *Kino, Teatras*
only spread gloom, like the violent graffiti
disdain has spray-painted on walls.

Round the back it's the same. Daubed slogans
compete with wet chipboard, damp ply
roughly nailed across window and vent

in this picture house lost to the stars,
the damp of the woods, all of its rustic pretence
slowly crumbling, like celluloid stock.

Rope Trick

Below his feet, the gaze of the earth
blurs over. All he sees is a whirlpool as the rotors
stir it up,

faces pricking the downdraft
with the whites of their eyes. And what little
they had saved,

stashed in a treetop or thatch. Nothing else,
till he spins
at the end of his line, bait

for their upraised arms, their hands that writhe
with pleading.
He needs them, he'll say,

like a hole in the head:
the one left by these rotting crops, drowned roads,
livestock floating belly up.

The cord jerks one more assisted birth
out of the flood. And he
winds down. They'll come in multiples from here.

An Executive Decision

Only murder shows up on time
faceless
>   behind its wire mask
afraid of itself
>   of its supple wrist
the rattle of bullets and teeth –
never late
>   it's just round the corner
in droves.

>   An engine turns over
men
>   (let's assume it is them)
kick down the tailgates
>   swarm
>   over kerbs
clear intersections
>   like doubt.

>   Nothing breaks bodies
that hasn't first smashed
>   the face
of the clock.
>   Shout louder
>   it finds you
your friends and relations.
Stay mum
>   you've invited it in.

from a line by Remco Campert

Mercenary

there is more in the bone
you'd bargain with

tissue and nerve
                    to make play
for the other man's goal

fibre and gut
in the absence
                    of purpose
of orders
            no-one will give
not a soul will graft
into places
                the mind
cannot go

            go spit
in another man's hand
press
        the flesh of the palm
        make the deal

Out-Station

Where we stopped the car was close enough to see
menace implicit in the raised palm of the fence,
its upper case commands that we go

no farther, take no photographs even of the view
we drove up this obscure road to see – the valley
from angles we'd never taken in before;

angles we suspect those busy in this block,
bland as it's anonymous, guess at in the merest blip
of radar, what some static might conceal; angles

as illicit as the view the man in uniform advancing
as we turn will do his damnedest to obscure
behind the gates of this out-station we don't wait

to be informed is out of bounds, but gun the throttle,
turn the blind eye of the tailgate on the place,
its guard a cipher in the mirror, logging our retreat.

Wake Up Call

The radio is on in the house next door
and, from this distance, the staccato Greek
echoing from concrete walls

sounds as alien as a spaceship
transmitting to Earth news
of our impending doom – a wake up call

as threatening as the thunder
still bilious in the peaks, lingering
from last night's storm. We'd woken then

to rain pounding the leaves,
torrents in the lane, the insistent banging
of shutters and doors as the wind

whipped them to life – a warning
we'd heeded long enough
to shoot the bolts, stumble feverish

back to bed, cursing the dreams
that plagued our sleep
and woke us to the white noise of dawn.

Dark Matter

I

It's the look of panic
glimpsed in freeze frame
moments before the fall,

legs a Catherine wheel
of thwarted hope
still spinning

against the gravity
that drops the body
from the cliff

seen too late to change
direction, hear
our muffled cry.

II

It's the silhouette
outlined in glass
whose jagged edges hint

at effort to stop in time,
limbs extended
to break momentum,

while speed and motion
hurl the object
of our attention

through the surface
only clocked
seconds before impact.

III

It's the figure invisible
but for a hat
suspended by illusion

in space
above the manhole
tumbled down,

attention wandering
from the present
lost now to this idler

deep inside our coal hole,
hatless, black, and bruised
by time and pace.

Copings

The Accents of Mice

Whinstone, rough as banter,
lets them in,

its grammar leaving space
for something

small enough
to pass as thought,

allowing sense
to mutter in the skirtings,

habits as ingrained
as accent in the brain

and harder than its markers
to expel.

As We Watch

Imagine the way the sun picks out
a house on a hillside,
a clump of trees apart from the wood

and makes them
shine like a blossom, a flare of petals,
like grass stems after rain;

or the way that light
can catch in a window, a bank of panes
on a building a distance off

and sign itself back, a message in code
guessed at by those who take time
to notice; time to stop

at a vantage point,
a bend in the road, and look
for import, some semblance of meaning

where it might be;
the way I found you that midnight,
stopped in my step by the light in your eyes,

their flare in the glow
of a single bulb, the message I read there
I'm living, and have still to live out.

Favour

In drinking tea your hand has brought,
I find, adhering to my gums,

no random leaf escaped from pot to tongue,
but this quite unexpected filament,

as russet, red-brown glowing as the Lapsang dregs
inhabiting the cup I put back in its place

to fumble round my teeth,
pluck out this strand of hair which curls

and springs back into shape. I turn it now
between my forefinger and thumb. Pale winter sun

picks out the highlights: yours. I store them up
in case the light fades or the cup is broken,

powers that drive my tongue
turn feeble, fumble for your hand,

as these words do I pluck now from the air.

In Passing

I wander, aimless through the house, to discover
you have left, on a table in the porch,
a plate of strawberries rescued from the rain;

the first downpour of August saying:
summer passes, fruits will rot
if not collected in the gaps between the showers;

and lying there, eight blood red hearts
still warm against the white cold of the plate,
they hold the pulse of seasons willingly;

willing me to take their musky sadness,
press it to my lips, tongue sweetness, tang and texture
as I pass them round the cold white of my teeth,

suck every tone and fibre of the balmy days,
lay it up against recurring downpours,
against the way we have of laying fruit upon a plate.

In the Flood

for Andy Goldsworthy

These stupa-like cairns that punctuate the gorge
are Goldsworthy's in spirit, if not
in name. We add to them

a stone, a pebble, waymarking the route
to lead those coming autumn will permit
the better down the course

of what will be a river come November
with the start of winter rain,
a torrent from the snow-melt in the spring.

The permanence of what resemble Henry Moores
in all their form and bulk,
shore up every fly-by-night route marker

stacked upon these eddy-sculpted rocks
but subject to the coming wash
of water Goldsworthy might welcome, were he here

in more than spirit, when the force
now dormant in the gorge sweeps all
direction, art, intention before it in the flood.

Diktamos Gorge, Crete

The Bitter Fruits

Something persuades the bitter fruits
that sweetness must be bought
with more than tears,

more than patience in the tending
of their needs, more than tasks
as endless as the seasons

still demand of those
who cut the stem to grow the shoot,
who risk the thorn

that worms into the flesh,
the gout of blood
that berries on the surface of the skin,

who cradle in the hollow of their palm
the thought of ripening,
something provable with time,

a certain knowledge
                    of vitality, of zest.

Spreading the Net

Rolled and stowed in the crooks of trees
since autumn, they find their purpose now:

a membrane stitched to terrace floors,
the sutures of this harvest. Meshed the way

that hands have plied one particular trade –
the loose weave cloth, the canvas netting

of their fathers' day – they take the ground
and pepper it with light, which flows

in plastic form, down hillsides cut to steps
beyond recorded time. We measure it –

our portion – spread upon the earth
and count its minutes in the steady drop

of olives, falling as we watch, on nets
like this one: open, wanting
                              like a palm.

Freeze

Perhaps Sunday is the reason
these sheep are nervously expectant,

their herd delayed at liturgy
sounding from the church below; more likely

late from bed, last night's christening
sending gunshots skyward

still in his head. Tensing at every vehicle
that follows the road, the beasts

line up by their trough, knowing the time
as perfectly as any clock,

and all stock still, their bells all silent,
heads all facing the gate,

they make their own classical frieze,
overlapping, sheep upon sheep,

fixed stares gazing millennia back, awaiting
the cornucopia they know will come

when morning wakes their shepherd,
and time fills up the trough.

Changeling

The ewes cry for their offspring
who've rejected them
in death

cry for the skin
flayed in mitigation
that's bodied round the orphan

(a swift nick, cut and peel)
thrusting one identity
all four legs

into the being of another
the mother
wiser than the moment

knowing hers
as more than this
still bloody from the knife

more than smell and touch
the thrust and nuzzle
of snout on teat

more than a cry
that echoes from the holding pen
draws out her response.

The Jaws of Wasps

A tinnitus so spare
it barely murmurs in the ear,

this steady graft
that rasps behind my back:

the jaws of wasps
fast wedded to these planks

flaked paint
has bared to their desire.

Each scart of timber they collect,
the work of fevered minutes,

leaves a track
dead wood can not repair;

but every minute builds
to hours, days, in time to this:

the bone-white byke
they'll hang from someone's eaves

to fizz with life,
an airy simulacrum of the brain.

Tree Surgeons

They range amongst the upper limbs
like primates encumbered with care,

find parts of trees we'd recognise
as human gestures on the level,

pass rope through crooks of elbows,
bends of knees, and anchor on

to laterals that bear the strain,
the dead weight of the saw

to make their surgery complete.
Down here, we're squinting at the sun

and, grounded by our lack of skill,
point out the deft incisions we require

to lighten up our lives. They make it so,
disguise it in the cut and pay down

branches, green and dying, each
a stretcher's girth, a sleeper's weight.

One Last Breath

Breaking a glass after how long – maybe twenty,
thirty years – since I chose it, old already,
from that junk shop shelf, I'm struck

that its one attraction has vanished too,
gone in the slip of accident, a moment's inattention
to where I placed my hand; and somewhere in the air

around the aftermath – brush and shovel,
the careful collection of shards – is what has escaped
from how old a prison I do not know:

a bubble of time sealed in the glass, released here
from what had confined it, the old air
mingling with now, but gone

in less than the beat of a pulse,
a whisper of wind as a corner is turned,
the barely expressed emission of one last breath.

History

It's paper still. Look, it holds its shape
lying on the coals, holds the print

read not a moment back, on white,
now black on grey, curling in the hearth.

It's lighter now. The updraft picks at edges
slowly crumbling into ash, picks at all

the history we toss as trivial to fires.
Look, we're courting dust. Our hands

will cast away perhaps a thousand words,
drop them all as easily as shedding skin.

Behind Your Eyes

There are times when you stop in your tracks,
halted by the scent of a blossom, the curve
of a particular leaf; times when these things

shift like the wind from absence to absence;
and all of you lurches forwards, foot before foot,
your mind one turn in the path from recognition

and this is one of these: a tree lies, particular of aspect,
along the way; a light blinks across the valley;
and darkness reaches out to touch you,

as this does, welling up from somewhere
you have been, you think, before but
did not know it, did not recognise the moment

that takes you now by something more
than just surprise; like something living, palpable,
that rustles in the underbrush, hides behind your eyes.

One for the Road

The headlights beam into the dark,
illuminating silence the vehicle moves into,

distant till it Dopplers past, a fan of light
that breaks upon a sky so full of stars

it's nothing but the swipe of us
intruding for a moment on the pitch of night

much as a match flares till it's shaken out,
or as we try to make our mark

but stumble, spill its substance, light up
our surroundings only briefly, see

there's nothing more than we'd steered into,
find we're fumbling for the map.

Notes on the Poems

Section Titles: 'Founding', 'Tracing', 'Hearting' and 'Coping' are terms specific to the various stages in the construction of a dry stone wall, respectively the foundation stones, stones built into the wall's sides, the in-filling stones, and the cap stones topping off the wall.

'The Tattie Line' (p. 22): The East Fife Central Railway, a branch line serving mines and farms, was closed in 1965. It ran from near Leven through the uplands of Fife terminating at Lochty. 'TK of old RLY' is the Ordnance Survey maps' abbreviation for 'track of old railway'.

'Sonny Rollins on the Williamsburg Bridge' (p. 32): In 1959, feeling pressured by his rise to fame, Rollins took a three-year break to focus on his craft. Hawk is the nickname of the saxophonist Coleman Hawkins. The term 'shedding' is jazz patois for time spent practising solo.

'The Method' (p. 33): A found poem based on extracts from an article by Alastair McKay (*The Scotsman*, April 2000). The Method is a series of techniques actors use to evoke internally the emotions of their characters in order to achieve lifelike performances.

'Making the Change' (p. 38): In the post-war period, up until the 1970s, primary school pupils received a daily bottle of school milk. This practice was ended by the then Secretary for Education, earning her the nickname 'Margaret Thatcher: milk snatcher'.

'Lady Day's Experience' (p. 46): The American jazz singer Billie Holiday, renowned for the emotional power of her delivery, was nicknamed Lady Day by her musical partner Lester Young.

'Contracted' (p. 52): Dupuytren's Contracture is an inherited tissue disorder of the palmar fascia of the hand in which the fingers bend towards the palm and cannot be fully extended.

It is named after Guillaume Dupuytren, the surgeon who described an operation to correct the condition in *The Lancet* in 1831.

'Zakros' (p. 62): Excavated in 1961, Zakros was the last of the Cretan Minoan Palaces to be discovered. The first excavations were made in the early 1900s by the British School of Archaeology but the ruins of the palace only emerged through later work by Greek archaeologist Nikolaos Platon.

'Tokens of Admission' (p. 64): The 2010-11 exhibition *Threads of Feeling* featured fabrics illustrating the moment of parting when mothers left their babies at the London Foundling Hospital. A small object or token, usually a piece of fabric, would be kept as an identifying record. For more information see www.foundlingmuseum.org.uk/PastExhibitions.php

'The Garment District' (p. 65): Based on an oral history recording featured in one of the tours at the Tenement Museum, New York City. For background see www.tenement.org/about.html

'Craiglockhart' (p. 66): The former Craiglockhart Hydropathic, used during the First World War for the treatment of shell-shocked officers, is now part of Edinburgh Napier University and houses their War Poets Collection. See www.napier.ac.uk/warpoets/collection.htm

'Sappers' (p. 67): During the First World War sappers tunnelling under enemy lines were frequently found to be suffering from photo keratitis or 'snow blindness' caused by exposure to light from their candles reflected constantly off the white surface of the chalky soil.

'How Well It Burns' (p. 68): In the voice of a Second World War German bomber pilot. For the filmpoem by Alastair Cook, with music by Rebecca Rowe, see http://vimeo.com/51247891#

'A Hotel in the Berenese Oberland' (p. 69): From the account of a 1947 visit with his mother to a hotel popular with rich pre-war tourists by Kevin Crossley-Holland, included in his memoir *The Hidden Roads*.

'An Executive Decision' (p. 74): The inspiration for the poem, and its first line, is from the poem *1944* by the Dutch poet Remco Campert, in the translation by Donald Garden.

'In the Flood' (p. 87): Andy Goldsworthy is a Scotland-based artist well known for his site-specific sculpture and land art. A wide range of photographs of his work can be found at www.morning-earth.org/artistnaturalists/an_goldsworthy.html

Author's Note

The author wishes to express his gratitude to John Glenday for his help and advice in the early stages of this collection, to Douglas Dunn for his appraisal of the finished version, to David Morley for his take on 'The Ring Cycle' sequence and to his editor at Arc, John Wedgewood Clarke, for his assistance in preparing the final manuscript. Very many thanks to Will Maclean for permission to use his work 'Star Chart' as a cover image.

Thanks to Richard Ingham for advice on the musical background to 'Sonny Rollins on the Williamsburg Bridge', to Peter Thomas for medical advice on 'Contracted', and to Alastair McKay for permission to use extracts from his article on Marilyn Monroe. Thanks also to Roddy Lumsden and Fiona Russell for checking details in 'Surfin' Safari for a Small Town Boy' and 'Changeling' respectively, and to Alan Donald for help with publicity material.

Thanks are also due to the Daskalaki family of Zakros in Crete for hospitality during the writing of a number of the poems in this collection and to everyone at Arc Publications for their backing. As always, the author is hugely indebted to his wife Jean Johnstone for her critical appraisal, her constant inspiration and unstinting support.

For more information see: brianjohnstonepoet.co.uk

Biographical Note

Born in Edinburgh in 1950, Brian Johnstone has lived in Fife since 1972. He was a primary school teacher in various Fife schools from 1975 to 1997 and from then until 2013 worked as a freelance arts organiser. He is now a full time poet, writer and performer.

Since returning to writing in the late 1980s, he has published two full collections *The Book of Belongings* (Arc, 2009) and *The Lizard Silence* (Scottish Cultural Press, 1996) as well as two pamphlet collections – *Homing* (Lobby Press, 2004) and *Robinson: A Journey* (Akros, 2000) – plus the CD *Storm Chaser* with his poetry, jazz and improv group Trio Verso. In 2009 a small collection of his poems in Italian translation was brought out by L'Officina (Vicenza).

His work has been published extensively in Scotland, elsewhere in the UK and in Europe and the Americas. His poems have been translated into more than ten different languages including Spanish, Catalan, Swedish, Slovakian & Lithuanian, and published in the respective countries.

In 2003 he won the Poetry on the Fringe competition at the Edinburgh Festival. Previous successes include winning the Writers' Bureau (2003) and the Mallard (1998) competitions, as well as being a prize winner in the UK National Poetry Competition (2000).

In 1998 he was a founder of StAnza: Scotland's International Poetry Festival, having previously co-founded Shore Poets in Edinburgh in 1991. He served as Festival Director of StAnza from 2000-2010 and has also taught creative writing for the Open College of the Arts and the University of St Andrews Department of Continuing Education.

Brian Johnstone lives with his wife, the maker of artists books Jean Johnstone, on the edge of the East Neuk of Fife.

Selected titles in Arc Publications'
POETRY FROM THE UK / IRELAND include: